The **V&A**
a souvenir

V&A Publishing

Contents

6   Welcome

_____

11   The **Museum**

73   The **Collection**

257 The **Unseen**

_____

319 Further information

320 How to use this book

322 Key resources

324 Further reading

Welcome

As the world's leading museum of art and design, the Victoria and Albert Museum (V&A) enriches people's lives by promoting the practice of design and increasing knowledge, understanding and enjoyment of the designed world. The Museum's collection was specifically intended, in its very earliest incarnation, to be a resource for students of art and design (see p.74), and, while the collections – and the museum itself – have transformed in the last century and a half, the ambition to inform and inspire remains unchanged.

The Museum was founded in 1852, following the enormous success of the Great Exhibition the previous year. Its founding principle was to make design available to all, and to inspire British designers and manufacturers. Profits from the Exhibition were used to supplement the fledgling collections of the Museum of Manufactures (as it was then known), then to buy the land on which the Museum currently sits and fund the construction of the first exhibition halls on this site (see p.12).

The newly renamed 'South Kensington Museum' was opened at the current site on 22 June 1857. Its collections expanded rapidly, as it set out to acquire the best examples of decorative art from all periods.

It also acquired fine art – paintings, drawings, prints, photography and sculpture. The Museum itself grew, with new buildings being added as and when needed. Many of these structures, with their iron frames and glass roofs, were only intended to be semi-permanent exhibition halls, but some survive as part of one of the finest groups of Victorian buildings in Britain.

In 1899, Queen Victoria laid the foundation stone of a new building, designed to give the Museum a grand facade and main entrance. It was renamed the Victoria and Albert Museum, in memory of the enthusiastic support Prince Albert had given to its foundation.

Since its nineteenth-century beginnings, the Museum has continued to grow and evolve, and is now home to an immensely varied and valuable collection of art and design, numbering over 2.25 million objects. In addition to the Museum at South Kensington, visitors can see the collections at the Museum of Childhood in Bethnal Green, dedicated to objects designed for and by children. As we move into the twenty-first century, further expansion is also underway at the V&A Museum of Design Dundee (due to open in 2018), and the V&A site in Stratford, East London (opening 2020).

These new ventures will allow the V&A's collections to be presented in exciting new ways, and will further expand visitor access to the day-to-day activities and holdings of the Museum.

This book is intended as a welcome to the V&A – an introduction to its collections, archives and the beautiful buildings in which it is housed. You can find out more about specific objects, events and experiences offered by the Museum by using the resources listed at the back. In the meantime, here are just a few of the sights you might encounter as you explore …

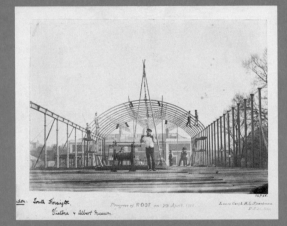

Lance Corporal B.L. Spackman
Exterior view of the roof of the South Kensington Museum
under construction (London, 1856)
V&A: 34966

The **Museum**

The first museum building to stand on the current V&A site at South Kensington (then the quiet village of Brompton) was also arguably the most controversial. In 1855, a government grant of £15,000 allowed the construction of the brick Sheepshanks Gallery and the 'iron house' to hold the collections of the government Museum of Manufactures (see p. 75). Made of corrugated iron, the infamous 'Brompton Boilers', as the new structures came to be known, were impractical and ugly, and were roundly criticized (a contemporary architectural journal declared of the building, 'its ugliness is unmitigated'). Accompanied from the outset by wooden buildings that housed the government Schools of Design, the 'Boilers' were joined in the late 1850s and early 1860s by a collection of architecturally disparate buildings built to display the ever-growing and increasingly varied collections of the Museum.

The first attempt at a rational, unifying masterplan for the Museum was made by Francis Fowke, a captain in the Royal Engineers. Unfortunately, Fowke died in 1865, before his careful planning could come to fruition, but he lived to see work begin on his 'Lecture Theatre building', which stands on the northern side of what is now the John Madejski Garden. Its grand facade was the original entrance to the Museum, and, in 1869, all that stood between it and Cromwell Road was grass. Above the bronze doors is the inscription 'Better is it to get wisdom than gold'.

Before he died, Fowke appointed designer and painter Godfrey Sykes to supervise the architectural ornament of his new buildings. Sykes himself died only three months after Fowke, but his students continued their work, alongside Museum Director Henry Cole and Fowke's successor, Colonel Henry Scott. These men oversaw some of the most spectacular features of the new building, including the ceramic staircase (designed by Frank Moody) and the breathtaking rooms that now form the Museum restaurant (pp.68–9). These were designed by Sir Edward Poynter, James Gamble and Morris & Co. respectively (the Morris Room was the first major commission won by Morris's fledgling company).

In keeping with Sykes's ambition that the project be a training ground for artists, many elements of the interior decoration were created, in the 1860s and early 1870s, by students (as well as the female convicts of Woking prison, who made mosaic floors for the staircase and Cast Courts).

Henry Scott was fired by the Office of Works in 1873, despite having dedicated nearly 10 years to the continuing building works. No further progress was made at the Museum until, in 1891, it was decided that a competition should be held to find a new architect and a new plan for the site. The winning architect was Aston Webb, whose design was praised for its grand, airy gallery spaces and sympathetic relationship with surrounding buildings. However, Webb's plan was subject to continual interruption, revision and compromise over the coming years. By the time Edward VII finally opened the new Museum in 1909, many features of the original plan had been dropped, including a grand staircase leading to the upper floors and a landmark tower crowning the southern facade. Some of the quirks of the Museum's current layout can be traced back to changes that Webb was forced to accommodate.

However, its current form – gradually lighted upon, as the formerly cavernous gallery spaces have been broken down into smaller rooms – provides a unique stage on which to surprise and delight visitors, with new collections and new vistas around every turn. The galleries, organized according to social and historical context, and materials on the upper floors, bring objects from different disciplines together with large-scale and architectural material. Building and collection complement and enliven one another in turn.

The Museum continues to evolve as it develops its 'Futureplan' – an ambitious programme of development that is transforming the V&A at South Kensington. The best contemporary designers are creating exciting new galleries and visitor facilities, while revealing and restoring the beauty of the original building. Over the past 10 years, over 70% of the Museum's public spaces have been transformed, including the Fashion Courts, Photographs Gallery and spectacular Ceramic Study Galleries on the fifth floor, in which 26,500 objects are displayed to form an 'encyclopedia' of international ceramic history.

Further detail about the history of the V&A buildings can be found on the Museum website at **vam.ac.uk/page/history** *and in the histories by John Physick (1982).*

The South Kensington Museum (now the V&A) was the first museum in the world to provide a public restaurant.

The South Kensington Museum was the first in the world to use gas lighting in the galleries, to allow for evening opening.

RUSSIA · DENMARK · SWITZERLAND · TURKEY

ALBERT CONSORT

THE FIRST EXHIBITION OF THE WORKS OF INDU

BELGIUM HOLLAND EGYPT PRUSSIA

OF QUEEN VICTORIA

Y OF ALL NATIONS : ANNO DOMINI MDCCCLI

READIN

G ROOM

Henry Cole's dog, Jim, and another 'faithful dog', Tycho, were buried in the V&A's garden – you can still see the plaques erected in their memory!

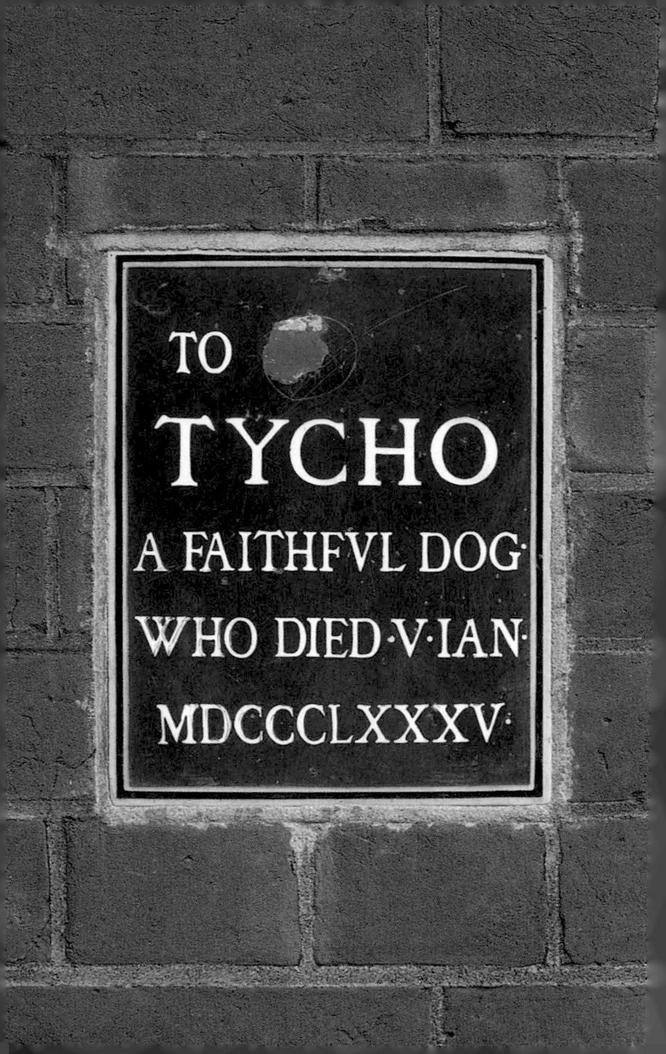

TO

TYCHO

A FAITHFVL DOG·

WHO DIED·V·IAN·

MDCCCLXXXV·

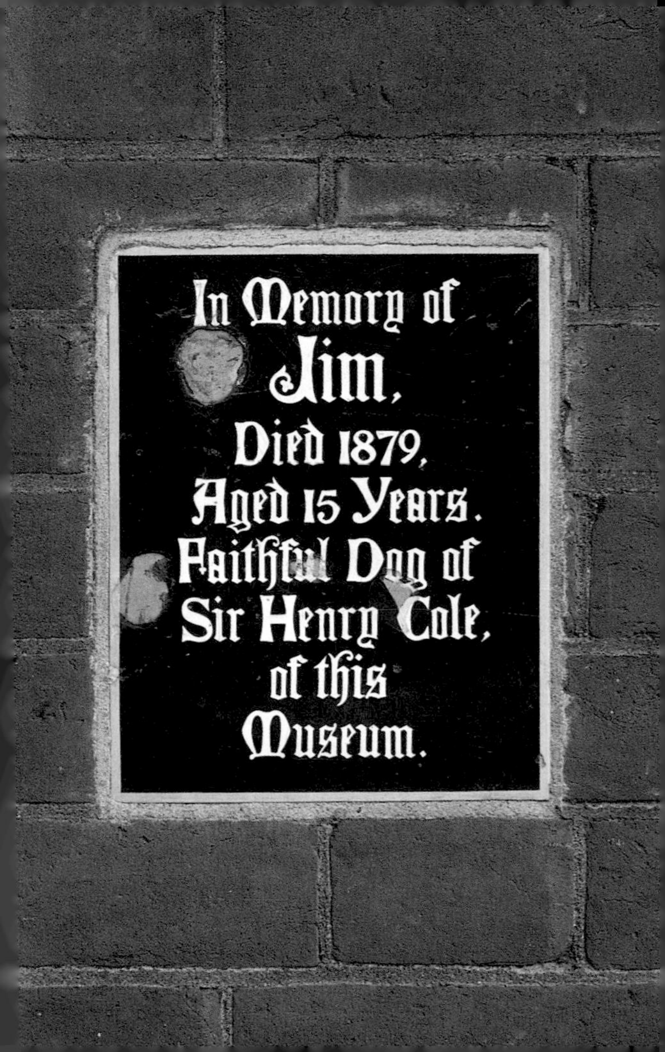

In Memory of
Jim,
Died 1879,
Aged 15 Years.
Faithful Dog of
Sir Henry Cole,
of this
Museum.

The statue on top of
the central tower of the
V&A – representing
Fame – is missing
her nose.

During World
War II, when most
of the collections
were evacuated, the
Raphael cartoons
(pp.154–5) were too fragile
to move and were
bricked up into a
protective shelter
on site.

Bolas & Co. / Victoria and Albert Museum
Gallery 40, View of Octagon Court
(London, England, c.1911)
V&A: E.1118–1989

The **Collection**

The V&A collections can seem incomprehensibly vast
and varied to the modern-day visitor, with holdings
ranging from 3000 BC Chinese celadon wares to
contemporary theatrical costume, from Antonio
Canova's celebrated sculpture of the Three Graces
(pp.224–5) to the oldest – and probably most beautiful
– carpet in the world (pp.138–9). Treasures held at the
Museum include the wedding suit of James II, Charles
Dickens's pen and several of Leonardo da Vinci's
notebooks (the Forster Codices, p.82). Many cutting-
edge, contemporary design objects from around the
world are also to be found on display, and in this book.
The Museum's variety and eclecticism is at its core,
but can be initially daunting.

The Museum's founders and early administrators
found the collection equally unwieldy – it has been
referred to variously as an 'immense bazaar' (Prosper
Mérimée), a 'refuge for destitute collections' (Henry
Cole, first director of the Museum) and 'an extremely
capacious handbag' (Roy Strong, Director 1973–87).

Beginning as the educational collection of the
government Schools of Design in the 1830s – and
largely consisting of plaster casts of Renaissance
sculpture and architecture – the collection grew in

size and variety in 1852, when the newly-appointed director of the Schools, Henry Cole, was given £5,000 to spend on exemplary design objects from the previous year's Great Exhibition. This hoard formed the basis of Cole's Museum of Manufactures (later, the Museum of Ornamental Art), which opened in 1852 at Marlborough House with the purpose of improving 'public taste in design' and illustrating 'the application of fine art to objects of utility'. This collection moved to the present site in 1857, and formed the basis of the South Kensington Museum.

Despite Cole's 1863 injunction that acquisitions 'be confined to objects wherein fine art is applied to some purpose of utility, and that works of fine art not so applied should only be admitted as exceptions', the following four decades saw a wealth of material added to the collections. The V&A was the first Museum to acquire photography (and the first to hold an exhibition of photographs, in 1858). The collection contains the earliest known photograph of London, a view down Parliament Street from Trafalgar Square, which was taken by a M. de Ste Croix in 1839 (p.151). Substantial collections of British watercolours and eighteenth-century French decorative art were among the first transferred to the Museum in its early years, and the original collections swelled further with additions including the loan of the Raphael Cartoons (pp.154–5), the transfer of the India Museum's contents (the basis of the current South Asian collection) and the opening of the National Art Library.

The Museum collections have continued to grow and, as of 2014, comprise over 2.25 million objects. Of these, the 'Display Collections' – objects and works of art suitable for long-term gallery display – number 233,742, about a quarter of which are actually on show in the galleries at any one time (turn to 'The Unseen', p.257, to see some of the others). In addition, a programme of national and international loans, and a busy schedule of touring exhibitions, mean that V&A objects can often be seen well outside the bounds of the museum buildings in South Kensington. The collections are available to everyone.

Embracing architecture, fashion, photography, theatre and performance (the collections of the British Theatre Museum and the Museum of Performing Arts were transferred to the V&A in 1974), sculpture, contemporary design, ceramics, Asian art and design, furniture, textiles, jewellery and metalwork, these objects span the cultures of Europe, North America,

Asia and North Africa, and date from ancient times to the present day.

Where to start? You could explore the history of design in the British Isles – highlights include William Morris textiles (p.102), stunning Arts and Crafts furniture, and the enormous, three-metre-wide 'Great Bed of Ware' (p.114), built for a Herefordshire inn in about 1590 and capable of sleeping 12 people.
The East Asian collections are among the finest in Europe – in the Japanese collection (one of the largest in Britain) stunning contemporary ceramics and textile arts sit alongside nineteenth-century samurai armour and delicate netsuke (pp.142–3).

Wherever you start, and wherever you end up, the collections invite you to be inspired, intrigued and surprised at every turn. There are also daily tours, and a constantly changing programme of exhibitions that enhance and expand the permanent collections.

Count Gleichen
Bust of Queen Victoria
(England, 1888)

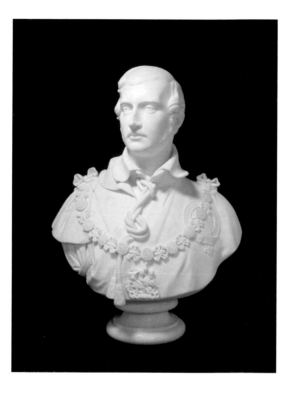

Edward Hodges Baily
Bust of Albert, Prince Consort
(London, England, 1841)
V&A: A.34–1964. Purchased with the bequest of Miss Ellen Barber.

V&A Bodoni typeface

A B C D E F G H I J K L M N
O P Q R S T U V W X Y Z & .

&A V&A   64 pt

Aboud Sodano
Contribution to V&A 150th anniversary album
(England, 2007)
V&A: E.477:1–2008. Given by the artist.

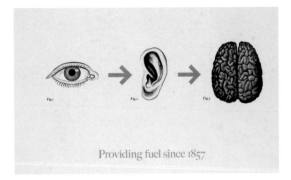

Providing fuel since 1857

Mike Dempsey
'Providing fuel since 1857',
contribution to V&A 150th anniversary album (England, 2007)
V&A: E.477:45–2008. Given by the artist.

Leonardo da Vinci
The Forster Codex, vol. II (62v–63r)
(Italy, late 15th–early 16th century)
National Art Library: Forster MS.141

'V&A – you really are
a national treasure.'

– Terence Conran

John Egan
Harp
(Dublin, Ireland, c.1820)
V&A: 332–1882

Abram Games (for Arthur Guinness Son & Co. Ltd)
'Guinness' poster
(Great Britain, 1957)
V&A: E.312–1981

Hannong's pottery factory
Tureen
(Strasbourg, France, c.1754–62)
V&A: C.211&A–1951. Bequeathed by Stuart Gerald Davis.

P. Croce
Costume design for the ballet *Amor*
(Italy, late 19th century)
V&A: S.354–2001. Cyril W. Beaumont Bequest.

Unknown maker
Boots from a theatre costume
(England, early 20th century)
V&A: S.535&A–1979. Given by the Scouts Association.

Unknown maker
Socks
(China, c.1880–1900)
V&A: FE.401:1, 2–2007. Given by Jill Proctor.

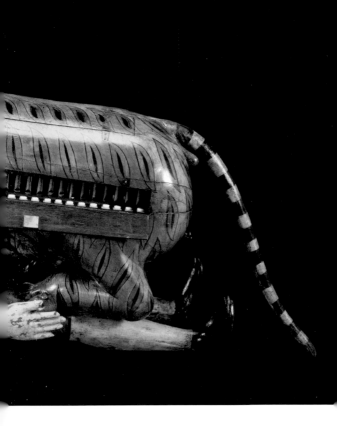

'Tipoo's Tiger' automaton
(Mysore, India, c.1793)
V&A: 2545(IS)

Edvard Munch (printed by Lassally)
The Kiss (fourth version)
(Berlin, Germany, 1902)
V&A: E.5067–1960

Kate Moss (published by SHOWstudio)
'Lipstick Kiss' (London, England, 2001)
V&A: E.1097:41–2002.
Purchased through the Julie and Robert Breckman Print Fund.

Reinhold Vasters
Pendant
(Aachen, Germany, *c.*1860)
V&A: 696–1893

Robert Bonfils (for Bianchini-Férier)
L'Afrique furnishing fabric
(Lyon, France, 1925–8)
V&A: CIRC.170–1932

Edward Raby (for Pountney & Co. Ltd)
Model of a bird's nest
(Bristol, England, c.1850)
V&A: C.620–1935. Bequeathed by Herbert Allen.

Ron Fuller
Egg-laying hen toy
(England, 1980s)
V&A: MISC.50-B–1988

The Shannongrove Gorget
(Ireland, 8th century BC)

V&A: M.35–1948. Given by Col. C.K. Howard Bury.

'A day's exploration of the V&A reminds us that time was once abundant.'

– *Nicholas Grimshaw*

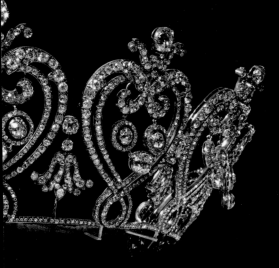

Cartier
Manchester Tiara (Paris, France, 1903)
V&A: M.6:1–2007. Accepted by HM Government in Lieu of Inheritance Tax and
allocated to the Victoria and Albert Museum, 2007.

William Morris
Acanthus wallpaper
(London, England, 1875)
V&A: E.496–1919. Given by Morris & Co.

Walter Crane
Swan, Rush and Iris wallpaper design
(England, 1875)
V&A: E.17–1945. Given by Mrs Margaret Warner.

Dong Nguyen (for GEARS Studios)
'Flappy Bird' app
(Hanoi, Vietnam, 2013)
V&A: CD.27–2014. Given by Dong Nguyen.

Peter Ghyczy (for Elastogran GmbH)
Garden Egg Chair
(Germany, designed 1968, manufactured 1971)
V&A: W.8–2007

The Becket Casket
(Limoges, France, c.1180–90)
V&A: M.66–1997

Purchased with the assistance of the National Heritage
Memorial Fund with contributions from the Po Shing Woo
Foundation, The Art Fund, the Friends of the V&A, the estate
of T.S. Eliot, the Headley Trust and many private donations.

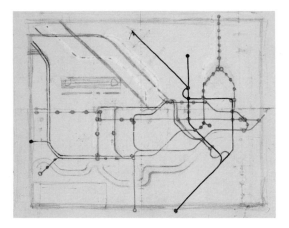

Harry Beck
Original sketch for the London Underground Railways Map
(London, England, 1931)
V&A: E.814–1979. Given by Ken Garland Esq.

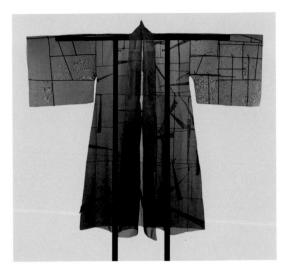

Chunghie Lee
Durumagi (overcoat), presented at *Fashion in Motion*, 2001
(Korea, 2000)
V&A: T.238–2001. Given by Chunghie Lee.

The Danny Jewel
(England, c.1550)
V&A: M.97–1917. Bryan Bequest.

The Burghley Nef, salt cellar
(Paris, France, 1527–8)
V&A: M.60–1959.
Supported by The Art Fund (Cochrane Trust) and The Goldsmiths' Company.

Robert Howlett
*Isambard Kingdom Brunel and the launching chains
of the* Great Eastern *(UK, 1857)*
V&A: PH.246–1979

Archie Brennan (for Dovecot Studios)
'Chains', from *Tapestries for the Nation*
(Edinburgh, Scotland, 1974–5)
V&A: T.187–1979

The Great Bed of Ware
(England, 1590–1600)

'I loved the V&A and still do ... of course my absolute favourite is The Great Bed of Ware. It sleeps 7 very comfortably. Every time I pass it, it makes me want to curl up and go to sleep.'

– Tracey Emin

Unknown maker
Camouflage suit, t-shirt and boots
(Germany/USA, 1988)
V&A: T.1023-5-1994; T.484A&B-1994

Edward Wadsworth
Camouflaged ships in dry dock ('Dazzle ships') (UK, 1918)
V&A: E.4139–1920

Dieter Rams (for Braun AG)
TP1 portable record player and radio
(Germany, 1959)
V&A: W.28:1-3-2008

Alexander Schervashidze, after Pablo Picasso
Front cloth for the ballet *Le Train bleu*
(Paris, 1924)

Unknown maker
Spacehopper
(UK, 1970s)
V&A: B.18–2001. Given by Sandie Cox.

Gareth Pugh
Ensemble presented at *Fashion in Motion*
(V&A, London, 2007)

Plaster cast of Trajan's column
(Paris, France, c.1864)
V&A: REPRO.1864–128

Tadanori Yokoo
'A la Maison de M. Civecawa', poster
(Japan, 1965)
V&A: E.43–2011

Andrew Grima
Brooch
(London, England, 1967–8)

V&A: M.34–2009. Given by William and Judith Bollinger.

Keppel Archibald Cameron Cresswell
Photograph showing a topographical view of Cairo, Egypt
(Egypt, 1916–21)
V&A: 2160–1921. Purchased from Professor K.A.C. Cresswell, 1921.

Unknown maker
Wedding dress
(England, 1857)
V&A: T.10A–C–1970. Given by the Misses I. and N. Turner.

Owen Jones
Original drawing for *The Grammar of Ornament*
(England, 1856)
V&A: 1618

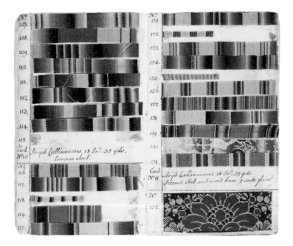

John Kelly (for Stannard, Taylor and Taxtor)
Pattern book
(Norwich, England, 1763)
V&A: 67–1885. Given by Mrs Bland.

Wedgwood
Portland Vase (Etruria, England, *c.*1790)
V&A: 2418–1901.
Transferred from the Museum of Practical Geology, Jermyn Street.

'A brilliant warehouse
full of design icons.'

– Richard Rogers

Jamie Reid, Malcolm McLaren and Vivienne Westwood
T-shirt modified and worn by Johnny Rotten
(London, England, 1976)
V&A: S.794–1990

Corinne Day
Kate Moss for *The Face* (July 1990)
(England, 1990)
V&A: E.75–1997

Defense Distributed (parts produced by Digits2Widgets for V&A)
'The Liberator' 3D-printed Hand Gun
(Texas, USA, 2013)
V&A: CD.1:1-17–2013

Robert Foster
TP49 teapot
(Queanbeyan, Australia, 2004)
V&A: M.2–2006

Gibson Les Paul
Guitar broken onstage by Pete Townsend
(1960s)

V&A: S.12–1978. Given by Allan Smith & Pete Townsend through John Entwistle.

Unknown maker
Khanjar (dagger)
(Mughal Empire, c.1580–1600)
V&A: IS.86–1981

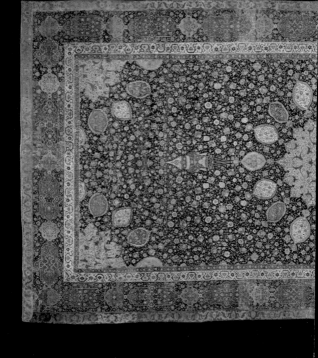

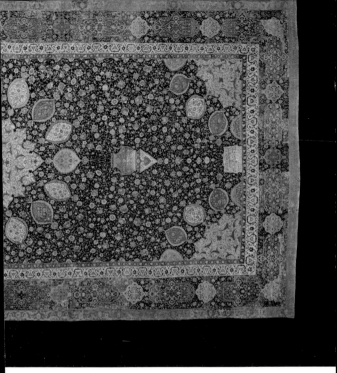

The Ardabil Carpet
(Iran, 1539–40)
V&A: 272–1893

Unknown maker
Salver tray
(Sheffield, England, late 18th century)
V&A: M.320–1912

Ford Motor Company
Car wheel trim
(England, 1991)
V&A: M.10–2005. Given by Ford Motor Company.

Unknown maker
Netsuke
(Japan, c.1750–1850)
V&A: A.59–1952. Shipman Bequest.

142

Reigyoku
Netsuke
(Japan, 1850–1900)

V&A: 564–1904. Dresden Bequest.

Deborah H. Harding
Vase
(England, *c.*1937)
V&A: CIRC.311–1954

Barbara and Zafer Baran
Dianthus #135 (Flower Cabinet)
(Richmond, England, 2003)
V&A: E.344–2005. Given by the photographers.

Tejo Remy
You Can't Lay Down Your Memories, chest of drawers
(Netherlands, designed 1991)
V&A: W.39:1-22–2008

'The V&A for me is
the perfect museum –
a great treasury, rich in
both artefacts and ideas.
What better place could
there possibly be to seek
inspiration or simply idle
away an afternoon?'

– Norman Foster

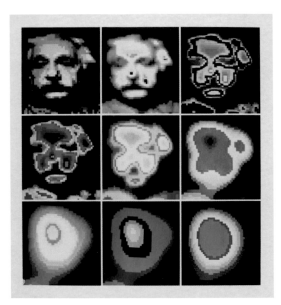

Herbert W. Franke
Elektronischer Einstein (Electronic Einstein) (Germany, 1972)
V&A: E.69–2008. Given by the Computer Arts Society,
supported by System Simulation Ltd, London.

Josef Albers (published by Ives-Sillman Inc.)
'Variant VI', from the suite of ten plates *Ten Variants*
(Connecticut, USA, 1969)
V&A: E.59:6–1994. Given by the Josef Albers Foundation.

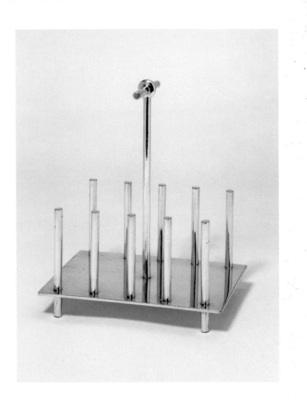

Christopher Dresser (for Hukin and Heath)
Toast rack
(Birmingham, England, manufactured 1878)
V&A: M.14–2005

M. de Ste Croix
Parliament Street from Trafalgar Square
(London, England, 1839)
V&A: PH.1–1986

Unknown maker
Model of a boat
(Guangzhou, China, c.1800)
V&A: A.6–1936. A.J. Hall Bequest.

Utagawa Kuniyoshi
A View from under the Shin-ohashi Bridge, from *Thirty-six Views
of Mount Fuji from Edo* (Japan, 19th century)
V&A: E.2266–1909

Raphael
The Death of Ananias (Acts 5: 1-5)
(Italy, *c*.1515–16)
V&A: ROYAL LOANS.5. On loan from the collection of Her Majesty the Queen.

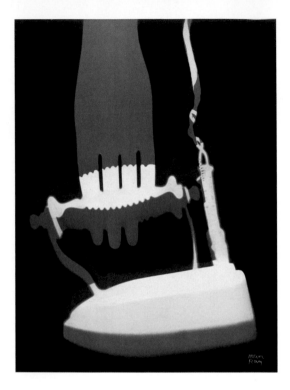

Man Ray (published by Compagnie Parisienne
de Distribution de l'Électricité)
'Lingerie', from the portfolio *Eléctricité* (France, 1931)
V&A: E.1646–2001. Purchased with the assistance of
The Art Fund and the Friends of the V&A.

Anna Atkins
Papaver Orientale (Poppy), from *Cyanotypes of British
and Foreign Flowering Plants and Ferns*
(UK, 1852–4)
V&A: PH.381–1981

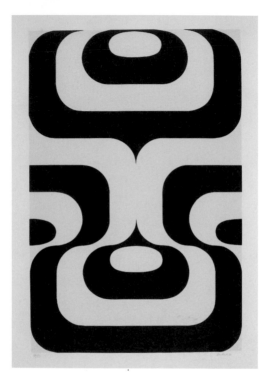

Manuel Barbadillo
Sin Titulo (Untitled) (Spain, 1972)
V&A: E.99–2008. Given by the Computer Arts Society, supported by System
Simulation Ltd, London.

Verner Panton (for Herman Miller Int.)
Panton Chair
(Basel, Germany, designed 1960, manufactured 1968)
V&A: CIRC.74–1969

Unknown maker
'Death' statuette
(Germany, 18th century)
V&A: A.2–1951. Given by Dr W.L. Hildburgh FSA.

Ester Hernandez
Sun Mad
(San Francisco, USA, 1982)
V&A: E.42–2014

Lulu Guinness
'Florist's Basket' handbag
(UK, designed 1993)
V&A: T.128–1996. Given by the designer.

'Dear V&A, the day
you asked to have
my Rose Basket Bag
in your permanent
fashion collection
– I knew I could be
knocked down by a
bus and my life would
have amounted to
something I could
be proud of!'

– Lulu Guinness

John Miers
Silhouette portrait of Isabella Burrell (England, late 18th century)
V&A: P.82–1929. Bequeathed by Miss Grace Valentine Stephenson
as part of the R.H. Stephenson Bequest.

Léonard Limosin
Medallion
(Limoges, France, c.1530–40)
V&A: 7912–1862

Edward William Godwin (for William Watt & Co.)
Sideboard
(London, England, 1867–70)
V&A: CIRC.38:1-5-1953

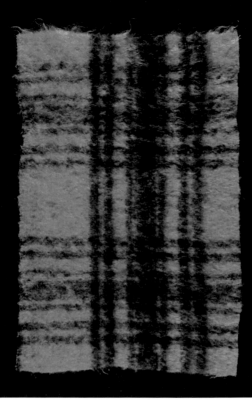

Ascher Ltd
Dress fabric
(UK, 1957)
V&A: T.196–1988. Given by Zika Ascher.

l'esprit humain l'artiste doit apporter toute son énergie, sa sincérité et la modestie la plus grande pour écarter pendant son travail les vieux clichés

90

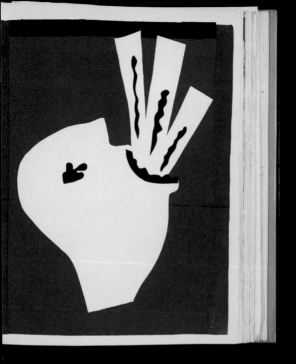

Henri Matisse
'L'Avaleur de Sabres' (Sword swallower), from *Jazz*
(Paris, *c*.1947)
National Art Library: L.338–1948

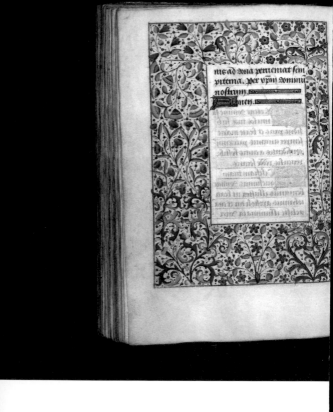

me ad bona perueniat sempiterna. Per eundem dominum nostrum.

Amen.

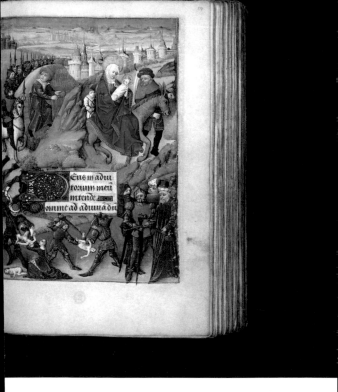

'The Flight to Egypt', from **The Margaret de Foix Hours** (83v–84r)
(France, c.1470)

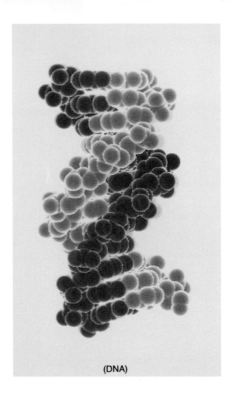

(DNA)

David Burder
DNA in 3D
(UK, 1989)
V&A: E.1392–1989. Given by David Burder.

Cyril Edward Power
The Tube Staircase
(London, England, 1929)
V&A: E.76–1981

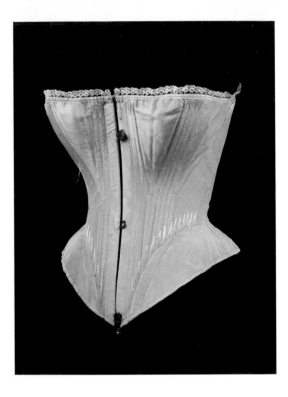

Unknown maker
Corset
(possibly France or UK, 1864)
V&A: T.169–1961. Given by the Burrows family.

Unknown maker
Armlet
(Egypt, 2nd century AD)
V&A: 631–1884

Sebastian Brajkovic
Lathe Chair VIII (Netherlands, 2008)
V&A: W.41–2008.
Purchased after a generous award from the Moët-Hennessy-DesignArt London Prize

Robert Adam (made by Thomas Chippendale)
Armchair (with modern upholstery)
(London, England, 1764–5)
V&A: W.1–1937

Harry Bertoia (for Knoll International)
Diamond Chair
(USA, designed 1952)
V&A: CIRC.82–1969. Given by Form International.

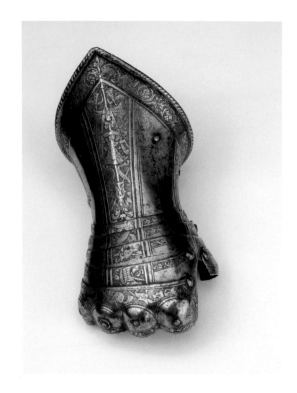

Unknown maker
Gauntlet
(Italy, c.1580)
V&A: M.466–1927. Bequeathed by Major Victor Alexander Farquharson.

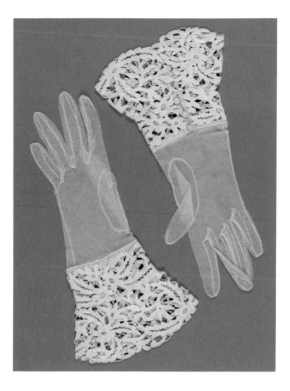

Unknown maker
Pair of ladies' gloves
(probably France, c.1935)
V&A: T.67&A–1977. Given by Cecil Beaton.

Jean Rousseau
Watch
(Geneva, Switzerland, 1660–70)
V&A: 2374–1855

Max Bill (for Uhrenfabrik Junghan)
Kitchen wall clock
(Schramberg, Germany, designed 1956)
V&A: M.224–2007

Unknown maker
Betel box and stand (Mandalay, Myanmar, 1875–1900)
V&A: IS.246&A–1964. Given by the Government of Burma,
pp H.E. U. Hla Manly, Ambassador of Burma, London.

'You [V&A] have been a source of constant inspiration. Long may you rule!'

– *Anya Hindmarch*

Unknown maker
Noh mask of Amazakuro Akujo
(Japan, 18th century)
V&A: 578G–1886

Unknown maker
Carved head of St John the Baptist
(England, 1470–90)
V&A: A.79–1946. Given by Dr W.L. Hildburgh FSA.

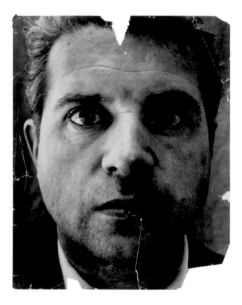

John Deakin
Francis Bacon
(England, 1952)
V&A: PH.100–1984

Ruth Gill et al. (for the Egg Marketing Board)
Poster
(UK, c.1964)
V&A: E.309–2011

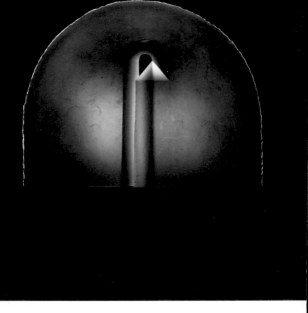

Stanislav Libensky and Jaroslava Brychtová
Arcus 1
(Zelezny Brod, Czechoslovakia, 1991)
V&A: C.4–1993.

Unknown maker
Grave tablet
(Germany, 1493)
V&A: M.27–1953. Given by Dr W.L. Hildburgh FSA.

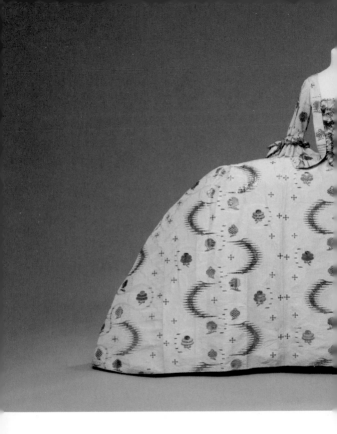

Unknown maker
Mantua
(England, 1755–60)
V&A:T.592:1-7-1993. Given by the Crawley Family.

William Hogarth
'The tavern scene', from *The Rake's Progress*
(England, 18th century)
V&A: DYCE.2727.
Bequeathed by Rev. Alexander Dyce.

Yinka Shonibare
Diary of a Victorian Dandy: 19.00 hours
(Herefordshire, England, 1998)
V&A: E.238–2013. Purchased with the support of the National Lottery through the
Heritage Lottery Fund and the Photographs Acquisition Group.

Haruta Tamba and Myochin Kunimichi
Suit of armour
(Japan, 1741)
V&A: M.979:1–1928

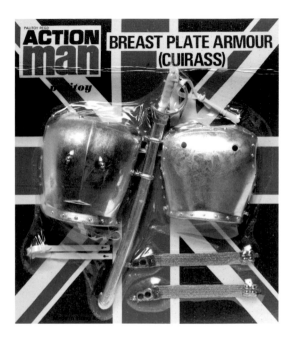

Palitoy Co.
Action Man 'Breast Plate Armour (Cuirass)'
(Hong Kong, 1970)
V&A: B.530–1994

Unknown maker
Chopines
(Venice, Italy, c.1600)
V&A: T.48&A–1914

Unknown maker
Qabâqib
(Egypt, 19th century)
V&A: 907+A–1884

Auguste Rodin
The Prodigal Son
(France, c.1885–7)

V&A: A.34–1914. Given to the Victoria and Albert Museum by Rodin in 1914.

'The V&A … a place to dream, study, admire and be inspired by things that human beings have made, sometimes from necessity, sometimes from joy. The V&A is a vast store-room full of possibility'

– Antony Gormley

Unknown maker
Brooch
(Germany, 1880s)
V&A: M.111–1977. Given by Mrs John Hull Grundy.

Arthur Silver (for Liberty & Co. Ltd)
Peacock Feathers furnishing fabric
(London, England, 1887)

V&A: T.50–1953. Given by Rex Silver, Esq.

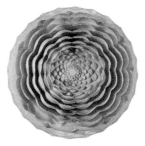

Hans Holbein and unknown maker (ivory case)
Box in the form of a rose, with a miniature portrait of Anne of Cleves
(Europe, 16th century)
V&A: P.153:1,2–1910. Bequeathed by George Salting.

Bettina Von Zwehl
Made up Love Song, Part 7 (London, England, 2011)
V&A: E.49–2012. Purchased with the support of the Friends of the V&A and
the Cecil Beaton Fund.

Man Ray (published by Compagnie Parisienne
de Distribution de l'Électricité)
'La Ville' (Town), from the portfolio *Éléctricité* (France, 1931)
V&A: E.1651–2001. Purchased with the assistance
of The Art Fund and the Friends of the V&A.

Fred Zinnemann
Election Night, New York
(New York, USA, 1932)
V&A: E.1688–1989

'Deer Hunt', one of the **Devonshire Hunting Tapestries**
(Netherlands, 1440–50)

Dante Gabriel Rossetti
The Day Dream
(England, 1880)

Richard Billingham
Untitled, from the series *Ray's a Laugh*
(Birmingham, England, 1995)
V&A: E.1085–1996

Neville Brody
The Pope's Wedding/Saved by Edward Bond, Royal Court Theatre
(London, 1984)
V&A: S.3728–1994

Aleksandr Rodchenko
(published by Moscow State Literature)
Leaflet advertising a production of Vladimir Mayakovksy's *Klop*
(The Bed Bug) (Russia, 1929)
V&A: E.1282–1989

Mario Avati
Untitled print
(unknown, 1959)
V&A: E.223–1994. Bequeathed by Walter Strachan.

Unknown maker
Drinking vessel
(London, England, 1676)
V&A: 414:821–1885. Given by Lady Charlotte Schreiber.

Giambologna
Samson Slaying a Philistine
(Florence, Italy, 1560–2)
V&A: A.7–1954. Purchased with the assistance of The Art Fund.

'Very Amazing.'

– Paul Smith

Yves Saint Laurent
Cocktail dress, from 'The Mondrian Collection'
(Paris, France, 1965)
V&A: T.369–1974. Given by the designer.

Unknown maker
'Free Bobby and The New Haven Panther 9' poster (USA, *c*.1970)
V&A: E.1438–2004. Gift of the American Friends of the V&A; gift to the American
Friends by Leslie, Judith and Gabri Schreyer and Alice Schreyer Batko.

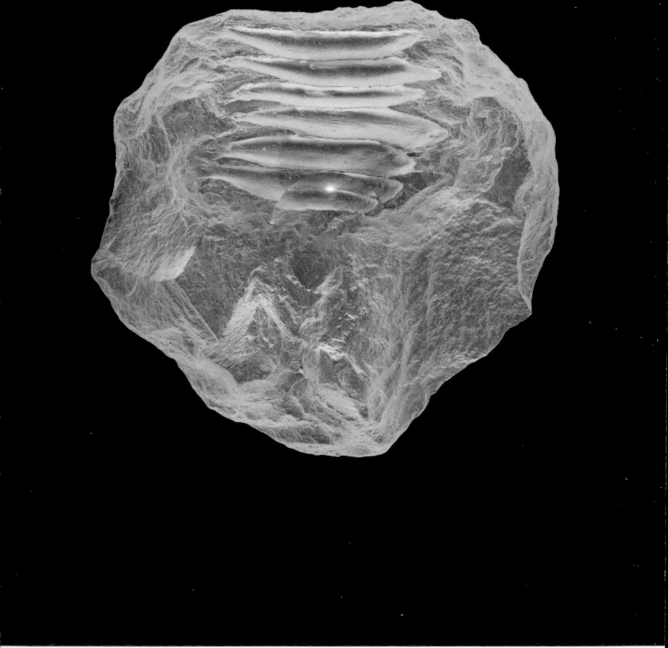

Colin Reid
'Ichthys' font
(Stroud, England, 2004–5)
V&A: LOAN:ACE.1–2005. Lent by the Art and Christianity Enquiry Trust.

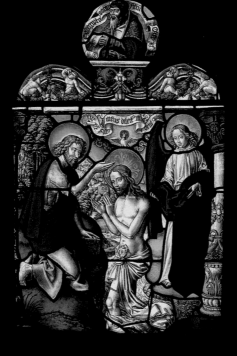

Master of St Severin
'The Baptism of Christ' stained glass panel
(Lower Rhine, Germany, c.1520–1)
V&A: C.311–1928. Given by Mr E.E. Cook.

Gavin P. Jantjes
'Untitled', from *(Zulu, the sky above your head)*
(UK, 1988)
V&A: E.1232–1995

LES CONSTELLATIONS. Nº 10. - L'ÉTOILE POLAIRE.

Unknown maker
'L'etoile polaire' (Polar Star) postcard
(France, *c*.1910)
V&A: E.523:83–2001. Given by Dr E. J. Dingwall.

Antonio Canova
The Three Graces (Rome, Italy, 1814–17)
V&A:A.4–1994

Purchased jointly with the National Galleries of Scotland, with the assistance of the National Heritage Memorial Fund, John Paul Getty II, Baron Heinrich Thyssen-Bornemisza, The Art Fund, and numerous donations from members of the public.

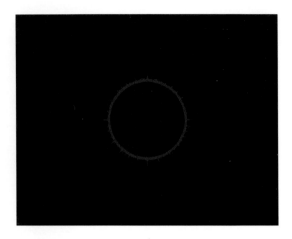

Garry Fabian Miller
Year One: Samonios
(Dartmoor, England, 2005–6)
V&A: E.1186:1–2012

Unknown maker
Drawing
(unknown, late 18th – mid-19th century)
V&A: E.478–2001.

Unknown maker
Brooch (unknown, 1875–1900)
V&A: M.196–2007. Gift of the American Friends of the V&A through the
generosity of Patricia V. Goldstein.

Per Arnoldi
Poster for the Paralympics, Atlanta 1996
(Denmark, c.1996)
V&A: E.361–2006. Given by Per Arnoldi.

Unknown maker
Brooch
(Europe, c.1880)
V&A: M.89–1977. Given by Mrs John Hull Grundy.

Solange Azagury-Partridge
'Hotlips' ring
(London, England, manufactured 2007)
V&A: M.22–2008. Given by Solange Azagury-Partridge.

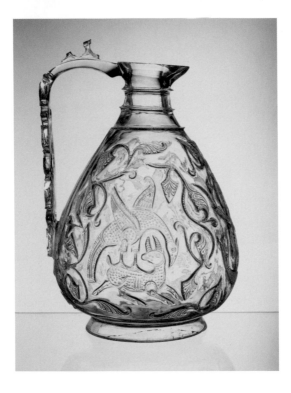

Unknown maker
Ewer
(Egypt, 1000–50)
V&A: 7904–1862

'The collections at the V&A never fail to intrigue and inspire me, the nation is privileged to have access to such a resource … it's the sort of place I'd like to be shut in overnight.'

– Alexander McQueen

Unknown maker
The Nuremberg Dolls' House
(Nuremberg, Germany, 1673)
V&A: W.41–1922

Moray Thomas et. al. (for William Purse)
'Whiteladies House'
(England, 1935)
V&A: W.3–1937

Dip Chand
Portrait of East India Company official
(Murshidabad, India, *c.*1760–4)
V&A: IM.33–1912

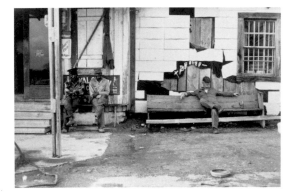

Henri Cartier-Bresson
Mississippi, 1961
(USA, 1961)
V&A: PH.682–1978

Jonathan Ive (for Apple Inc.)
iMac G3
(USA, designed 1998)
V&A: W.29:1-4–2008. Given by Philip Steadman.

Charles Rennie Mackintosh
Chair
(Glasgow, Scotland, c.1907)
V&A: CIRC.128:1, 2–1958. Given by the Glasgow School of Art.

John Constable
Study of Cirrus Clouds (England, c.1822)
V&A: 784–1888. Given by Isabel Constable.

Unknown maker
Portrait of King George V
(Delhi, India, c.1911)
V&A: IS.44–1979

Unknown maker
Hanging scroll
(Korea, 19th century)
V&A: FE.48:1–1993

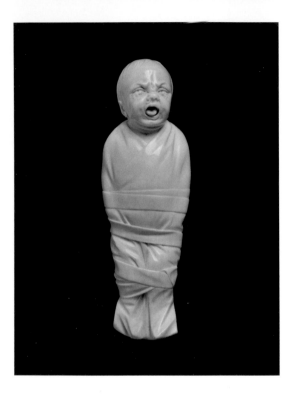

Johann Christian Ludwig von Lücke
Crying baby in swaddling clothes, statuette
(Germany, c.1753–5)
V&A: A.17–1954

Unknown maker
Torre Abbey Jewel
(England, 1540–50)
V&A: 3581&PART–1856

Unknown maker
Ring
(China, 2nd century BC)
V&A: A.44–1938

Unknown maker
Tile
(probably Kashan, Iran, early 14th century)
V&A: 1835–1876

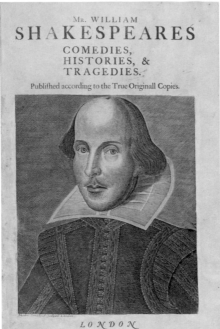

Printed by Isaac Jaggard and Edward Blount
William Shakespeare's first folio (London, England, 1632)
V&A: L.1392–1882.
Bequeathed by John Jones (1800–82) to the V&A National Art Library.

'Aside from the pleasure we get from looking at beautiful objects, we artists go to the V&A for sustenance.'

– *Anthony Caro*

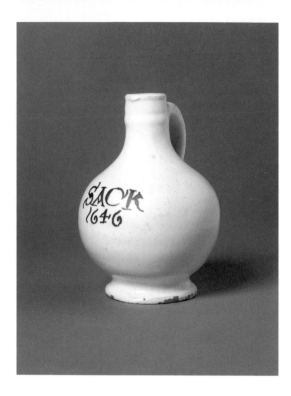

Unknown maker
Wine bottle (London, England, 1646)
V&A: 3876–1901. Transferred from the Museum of Practical Geology,
Jermyn Street.

Robert Brownjohn
Street Level
(London, England, 1961)
V&A: E.700–2012

Unknown maker
'Trench Football' game
(England, c.1914)
V&A: MISC.19–1973

Christopher Richard Wynne Nevinson
Returning to the Trenches
(UK, 1916)
V&A: CIRC.581–1966

View of packing case and horse-drawn van for transporting
Raphael Cartoons from Hampton Court, London,
to South Kensington Museum (London, England, 1856)
V&A: E.1090–1989

The **Unseen**

If you would like to investigate beyond the displays at the V&A or the V&A Museum of Childhood at Bethnal Green, or if you have a particular research interest that you would like to pursue, you can explore both the Display Collections (only about a quarter of which are actually on show at any one time) and the Reference Collections, which for conservation reasons can only be displayed for short periods. These objects may be 'unseen' in the context of a casual visit, but they are available to everyone. Seven main Study Rooms are open by appointment, for those who want to learn more (see p.323 for details), and the Museum provides regular opportunities for you to get curatorial opinions and or to make enquiries.

The following pages provide just a glimpse of the many objects and archives that are held by the V&A but not necessarily displayed. The Archive & Library Study Room provides public access to the Archive of Art and Design, the Beatrix Potter Collections, the V&A Theatre and Performance Archive and the V&A Archive itself, which contains a wealth of material relating to the institution. Alongside files relating to the architectural history of the Museum, its organization and holdings, you can access ephemera including exhibition posters, archival photographs and fascinating records of the Museum's hidden histories. Did you know, for example, that William Morris used to be an 'Art Referee' for the Museum, reporting on and recommending objects for acquisition; or that, during World War II, parts of the V&A served as a canteen for the Royal Air Force? The Museum's 'Tales from the Archives' website reveals these stories and more from across the archival holdings, with subjects including World War II uniform and dress, couture lookbooks and the history of early music performance at the Museum.

The Clothworkers' Centre for the Study and Conservation of Textiles and Fashion provides access to objects ranging from embroidery samples (pp.290–1) to avant-garde creations by the likes of twentieth-century designer Gareth Pugh (p.272); from eighteenth-century quilts to contemporary accessories.

At the V&A itself, prints and drawings (and paintings, and photographs); RIBA's architectural drawings and manuscripts; ceramics; and South and South East Asian objects can all be accessed in the Study Rooms and NAL.

The collections shown here may not be truly 'unseen', but the V&A is the site of many hidden facilities and histories and, of course, a great deal of ongoing behind-the-scenes work, devoted to the conservation, exhibition, storage and transport of the collection. The cutting-edge conservation and science facilities are showcased over the following pages, as the experts working there engage in their day-to-day activities, ranging from analysing the materials used to make an Egyptian sandal, to experimenting with nineteenth-century painting techniques, in order to better understand and conserve the Museum's collection; from conserving Chinese scrolls to writing public guidelines on how to care for your ceramics.

We hope that this tour of some of the V&A facilities and collections, beyond South Kensington and Bethnal Green, inspire your own journey of discovery among the collections.

Further information about the conservation work of the Museum can be found at **vam.ac.uk/page/c/conservation** *and you can see more about caring for your own collection at* **vam.ac.uk/page/c/caring-for-your-possessions/**

When deliveries were made to the Museum by horse and cart there was not enough room for drivers to manoeuvre; there was a large turn-table on which both horse and cart could be turned round.

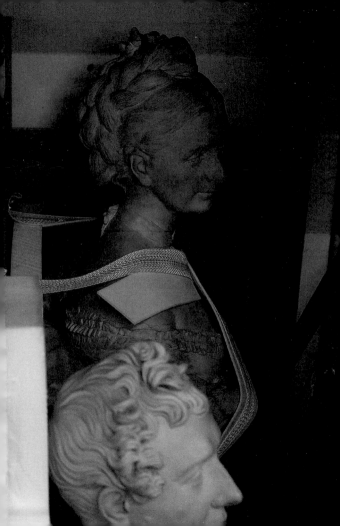

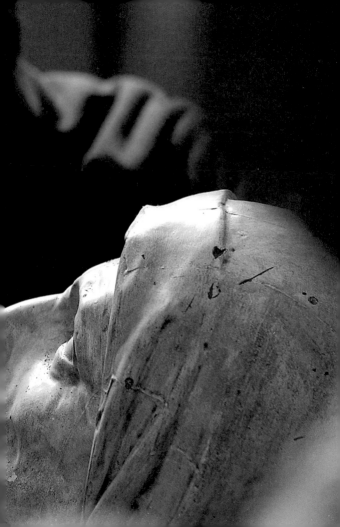

The inscription over
the main entrance
of the Museum reads
'The excellence of
every art must consist
in the complete
accomplishment of
its purpose' – a quote
from Sir Joshua
Reynolds.

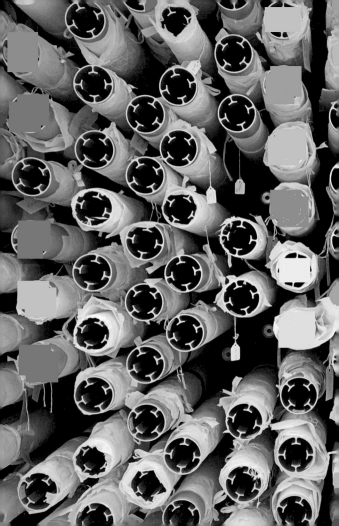

In the early 1980s, after
a flood in a basement
store, damaged books
were taken and put
in freezers at Harrods
department store until
they could be restored.

The V&A owns some of
Elton John's spectacles,
Adam Ant's jackets,
and Sandie Shaw's
Eurovision costume.

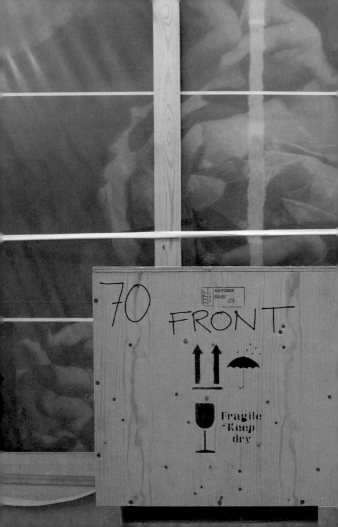

Many films have been shot at the V&A and at Blythe House, Olympia – look out for the freight lift at Blythe House in *Tinker Tailor Soldier Spy* (2011).

FRAGILE

Further information

How to use this book

Captions in the collection section of this book
take the following form.

Artist or maker
Description or title (place of manufacture or design, date)
Object number ('T.276–1974' or similar)
Acquisition credit.

If you would like to find out more about a particular
object, you can visit **collections.vam.ac.uk** and search
using the relevant object number.

As well as information about the maker, constituent
materials and history of any given object, the website
also gives its location in the Museum. Some objects
illustrated in this book are 'In storage', in which case you
may be able to arrange to view them in one of the V&A
Study Rooms (see overleaf) or through correspondence
with the relevant collections department.

For further information about researching the collections
at the V&A, the history of the South Kensington site, or
public access and events at the Museum, please see the
V&A website (links overleaf).

Key resources

Visiting the Museum
vam.ac.uk/visit

History of the Museum
vam.ac.uk/history

Seach the collections
collections.vam.ac.uk

Study Rooms
vam.ac.uk/study-rooms

Archives
vam.ac.uk/archives

The Clothworkers' Centre
vam.ac.uk/clothworkers

National Art Library
vam.ac.uk/nal

V&A Shop
www.vandashop.com

V&A Membership
vam.ac.uk/membership

Further reading

Elizabeth Bonython and
Anthony Burton
*The Great Exhibitor: The Life
and Work of Henry Cole*
London, 2003

Gregory Irvine (ed.)
Japanese Art and Design
London, 2015

Elizabeth Miller and Hilary Young (eds)
The Arts of Living: Europe 1600–1815
London, 2015

Halina Pasierbska
*Dolls' Houses from the
V&A Museum of Childhood*
London, 2014

Clare Phillips
Jewels and Jewellry
London, 2006

Rowan Watson, Elizabeth James
and Julius Bryant (eds)
*Word & Image: Art, Books and Design
from the National Art Library*
London, 2014

Claire Wilcox and Jenny Lister (eds)
V&A Gallery of Fashion
London, 2013

Sarah Wood
*Museum of Childhood:
A Book of Childhood Things*
London, 2012

Credits

First published by V&A Publishing, 2015
Victoria and Albert Museum
South Kensington
London SW7 2RL
www.vandapublishing.com

Distributed in North America by Abrams, an imprint of ABRAMS
© Victoria and Albert Museum, London

The moral right of the author(s) has been asserted.

ISBN 978 1 85177 876 8

10 9 8 7 6 5 4 3 2 1
2019 2018 2017 2016 2015

Endpapers: designs taken from tile patterns found at
the Victoria and Albert Museum, South Kensington

Design: PlanningUnit.co.uk

New photography by Jaron James, V&A Photographic Studio

Printed in Italy